THE POWER OF NATURE

# TORNADOES

Arthur Gullo

Cavendish
Square
New York

Published in 2015 by Cavendish Square Publishing, LLC
243 5th Avenue, Suite 136, New York, NY 10016

Library of Congress Cataloging-in-Publication Data

Gullo, Arthur.
Tornadoes / by Arthur Gullo.
p. cm. — (The power of nature)
Includes index.
ISBN 978-1-5026-0217-6 (hardcover) ISBN 978-1-5026-0216-9 (ebook)
1. Tornadoes — Juvenile literature. I. Gullo, Arthur. II. Title.
QC955.2 G85 2015
551.553—d23

Editor: Fletcher Doyle
Copy Editor: Cynthia Roby
Art Director: Jeffrey Talbot
Designer: Joseph Macri
Senior Production Manager: Jennifer Ryder-Talbot
Production Editor: David McNamara
Photo Researcher: J8 Media

The photographs in this book are used by permission and through the courtesy of:
Cover photo Cultura Science/Jason Persoff Stormdoctor/Oxford Scientific/Getty Images; Mario Tama/Getty Images, 4; AP Photo/tornadovideo.net, 7; AFP/Getty Images, 8; Shutterstock.com/Designua, 11; Mario Tama/Getty Images, 13; Hulton Archive/Getty Images, 14; Dan Craggs/File:Tornado Alley Diagram.svg/ Wikimedia Commons, 16; Gabe Garfield and Marc Austin/File:Tushka, Oklahoma tornado April 14, 2011.jpg/ Wikimedia Commons, 18; Jessica McGowan/Getty Images, 20; Handout/Getty Images, 24; Topical Press Agency/ Hulton Archive/Getty Images, 26; JOSHUA LOTT/AFP/Getty Images, 28; Mike Olbinski/Moment/Getty Images, 29; AFP/Getty Images, 30; Howard Bluestein/Photo Researchers/Getty Images, 32; NWS Tallahassee – http://www.srh.noaa.gov/tlh/svrwx030107/File:Enterprise Radar.jpg/Wikimedia Commons, 34; NSSTC Lightning Team/NASA, 35; Klaus Vedfelt/Iconica/Getty Images, 37; Jim Reed/Photo Researchers/Getty Images, 38.

Printed in the United States of America

# CONTENTS

Residents search for unbroken items in Joplin, Missouri, two days after a deadly tornado hit.

On May 22, 2011, a deadly tornado rocked the city of Joplin, Missouri. The damage and casualties were shocking. In total, 158 people were killed and more than one thousand others were injured. In addition, more than seven thousand homes, five hundred businesses, and numerous churches and schools were destroyed. The catastrophe amounted to billions of dollars in damages. Today, residents continue to rebuild their lives after one of the worst tornadoes in U.S. history.

The tornado touched down and remained on the ground for 6 miles (9.7 kilometers). Everything in its path was destroyed. While many tornadoes rip through an area quickly, this one was much slower, and its pace increased the damage it caused. The head **meteorologist** at Springfield's **National Weather Service (NWS)** station described the tornado as a "fist coming out of the sky."

Tornadoes, which are also called twisters, occur frequently in this part of the country. NWS issued a **tornado watch** for the area four hours before the twister touched down in Joplin. Thirty minutes before the storm hit, it was upgraded to a **tornado warning**. During a NWS investigation, it was concluded that many people responded to these watches and warnings, and lives were saved. Some people, however, did not take the warnings seriously and did not take appropriate safety steps.

Almost everyone in Joplin, a city boasting a population of fifty thousand, was affected by the storm. After viewing images of the devastation, citizens nationwide reached out to help. The federal government and private charities offered assistance. Volunteers from organizations such as Habitat for Humanity came to help rebuild homes. For some residents, however, it was too much to overcome. They chose to leave the area.

People often think only of the immediate damage caused by tornadoes. Such a storm can permanently alter the lives of those in its path, however. The long-term results can be traumatic for the victims, who may never again feel safe.

Lightning flashes inside the tornado that destroyed areas of Joplin.

A tornado turns debris into flying missiles that can cause severe damage.

# CHAPTER ONE
# POWERFUL TWISTERS

Over a two-day period in April 2014, a rash of tornadoes hit the Midwest and southern portions of the United States. The Midwest was hit with at least eleven tornadoes on April 27, and the South felt the wrath of at least twenty-five twisters the next day. More than thirty people died. In Alabama, three deaths occurred on the third anniversary of a spate of sixty tornadoes that ravaged the state and killed more than 250 people.

In Tupelo, Mississippi, business owner Francis Gonzalez took cover with her three children and two employees in her store's cooler as the roof over her gas station was reduced to aluminum shards. "My lord, how can this all happen in just one second?" she said to CBS News.

# Understanding Tornadoes

A tornado is a spinning column of air that touches the Earth's surface. Normally, you would not be able to see air, but tornadoes gather clouds and dust until its shape becomes clear. The whirling dust and clouds form a **funnel**. Inside the funnel, winds are moving at speeds of 40 to 318 miles per hour (64 to 512 kilometers per hour). These winds create a **vacuum**, sucking up everything in its path. Depending on its size and speed, a tornado funnel can move houses, bridges, livestock, and cars.

# Creating a Tornado

Tornadoes are produced by severe thunderstorms. For a tornado to occur, the thunderstorm has to have an exact balance of temperature, **humidity** (moisture), and wind. A **tornadic thunderstorm** is a storm capable of producing a tornado. A tornadic thunderstorm is created when warm, moist air is trapped under a layer of cold, dry air and another layer of warm, dry air. If weather conditions are right, the two top layers become unstable.

The bottommost layer of warm, moist air is then able to push through the layers above it.

The moist air is propelled upward by winds near Earth's surface. These winds also cause the air to rotate. The wind spirals quickly upward at speeds of up to 150 mph

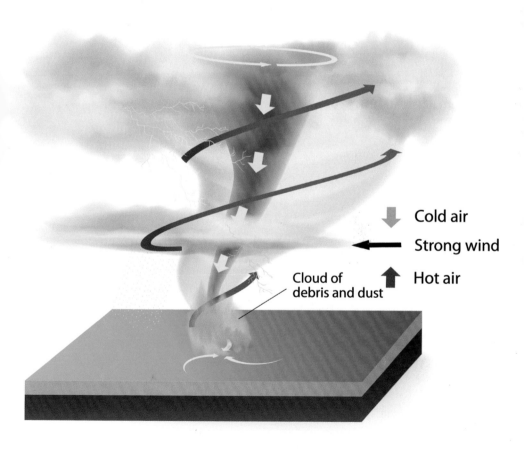

Cold air

Strong wind

Cloud of debris and dust

Hot air

Tornadoes need warm, moist air; cold, dry air; and strong crosswinds to form.

(241.5 kmh). The moist, swirling wind that blows up from the Earth's surface is called an **updraft.** The updraft is what fuels a thunderstorm and keeps it going. The stronger the updraft, the stronger the thunderstorm— and the more likely a tornado is to form.

As the air rises higher into the **atmosphere**, it begins to **condense** from a vapor, or gas, into a liquid, which falls as rain. This process produces a lot of rain, lightning, and heat. This heat is the main source of energy in a tornadic thunderstorm.

## DID YOU KNOW?

Florida experiences the highest number of tornadoes per square mile in the United States. It averages 12.3 tornadoes per 10,000 square miles (25,900 square kilometers) every year.

# The Time for Tornadoes

Tornadoes are reported every year in Australia, Brazil, Canada, Great Britain, India, Italy, Japan, and South Africa. Since weather patterns vary, certain areas have more tornadoes than others. The United States has a weather pattern that spawns an average of 1,200 tornadoes per year. This is more than any other country.

Storm clouds again gathered over Joplin, five days after the tornado in 2011.

Some tornadoes are shaped like ropes.

March through July is the peak tornado season in the United States. During those months, an average of five tornadoes touch down each day. Although they have occured during all times of day, tornadoes are most likely to occur in the midafternoon. Patterns for these occurrences are based on a combination of heat, wind speed, and

**air pressure**. Wherever there is warm and moist air, low air pressure, and shifting winds, there is a good chance that severe thunderstorms will form. These conditions usually are present in the spring months and late in the day—when there is more hot air in the atmosphere.

# The Different Types of Tornadoes

Tornadoes come in many shapes and sizes. Some are long and narrow like ropes, with winds of less than 50 mph (80.5 kmh). Others can be 1.5 miles (2.5 km) wide, with winds swirling at 300 mph (483 kmh). Some tornadoes take on the shape of an hourglass, while others resemble tall columns. Most tornadoes are funnel shaped, which means they are wide at the top and narrow at the bottom.

The average tornado funnel is about 800 to 2,000 feet (242–606 meters) tall. Most funnels are less than 1 mile (1.6 km) wide at the base (the tip that touches the ground). The average width at the base is about 600 to 900 feet (182–273 m). Some tips may be only 10

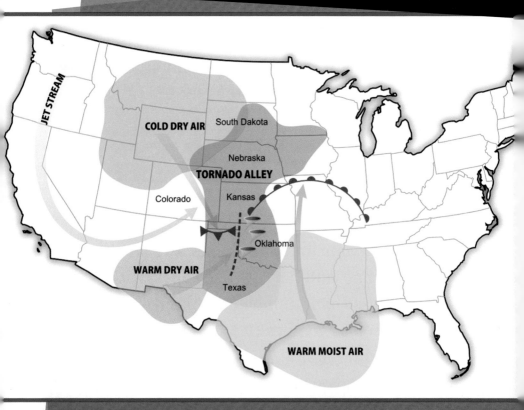

Geography and weather create Tornado Alley.

Most tornadoes occur in the central United States in an area called **Tornado Alley**. Tornado Alley stretches across several states, including Iowa, Kansas, Oklahoma, Missouri, Nebraska, and Texas.

All of the elements needed to form tornadoes, such as a mixture of warm and cold air, strong winds, moisture, and shifting winds, can be found in Tornado Alley. In spring, a weather pattern called the **jet stream** moves from the west and settles over the central United States. The jet stream brings with it strong winds and low air pressure. The low air pressure draws in moist air from the Gulf of Mexico. The combination of hot air, cold air, and shifting winds produces many severe thunderstorms. Such weather increases the chances for tornadoes to develop.

Tornado Alley has no real agreed-upon boundaries. The definitions of these boundaries depend on how tornadoes in each area are categorized (frequency, intensity, or number of events). A significant number of tornadoes occur in the South, so some people call the area in the lower Mississippi Valley and the Tennessee Valley "Dixie Alley."

feet (3 m) wide. When a tornado's tip is small, the damage is limited to a narrow path along the ground. The tornado may destroy one house completely, while leaving the house next to it untouched.

Sometimes a cluster of several tornadoes hits an area at the same time. This group of tornadoes is known as an **outbreak**. Outbreaks are far more dangerous and destructive than single tornadoes.

A multi-vortex tornado strikes Tushka, Oklahoma, on April 14, 2011.

# Killer Tornadoes

Certain storms will produce a large tornado that has several smaller tornadoes inside its large main funnel. This type of tornado is a **multi-vortex tornado**. Despite its name, it is a single storm.

Sometimes people call multi-vortex tornadoes, "killer tornadoes." This is because multi-vortex tornadoes have several funnels, are much larger and wider than average tornadoes, have wind speeds of up to 300 mph (483 kmh), and can cause far more damage than the average tornado.

Tuscaloosa suffered severe damage in the Alabama outbreak in 2011.

In late April 2011, the Midwest, South, and Northeast were hit with one of the deadliest tornado outbreaks in U.S. history. Over a four-day period, more than 350 deadly tornadoes hit these areas. States from Texas to New York experienced the storm's wrath. While 348 people overall in the storm's path were killed, the state of Alabama, with more than 230 deaths, was hit the hardest. Alabama was hit mostly on April 27, with sixty-two confirmed tornadoes, including twenty-nine in the Central Alabama region.

## The Fujita Scale

In 1971, Dr. T. Theodore Fujita developed a scale used for measuring wind speed, which links damage to estimated wind speed.

This scale is called the Fujita-scale, or the **F-Scale**. Generally, the United States is hit with an average of seven F4 or F5 tornadoes per year. The April 2011 storm, however, had eleven F4 tornadoes and four F5 tornadoes in one outbreak. It was estimated that the storms caused more than $6 billion in property damage.

This was by far the most devastating tornado event in history. It was even more damaging than the "Super Outbreak" of April 1974. That collection of twisters resulted in 330 deaths and more than five thousand injuries. However, it may have helped the country be better prepared for the 2011 outbreak. After the devastation of the 1974 outbreak, the country decided to invest more in storm forecasting technology and better warning systems. Meteorologists knew that another outbreak could occur, and less than forty years later, they were proven correct. The warning systems developed over the years may have saved countless lives in 2011.

# A Tornado's Movement

The movement of each tornado is different. There are some similarities, however.

| Fujita Scale | 3-Second Gust Speed (mph) | Enhanced Fujita Scale | 3-Second Gust Speed (mph) | Typical Damage |
|---|---|---|---|---|
| F0 | 45-78 | EF0 | 65-85 | Light: Some damage to chimneys; shallow-rooted trees pushed over. |
| F1 | 79-117 | EF1 | 86-109 | Moderate: Peels surface off roofs; moving autos blown off roads. |
| F2 | 118-161 | EF2 | 110-137 | Roofs torn off frame houses; light-object missiles generated. |
| F3 | 162-209 | EF3 | 138-167 | Severe: Roofs and some walls torn off houses; heavy cars lifted off the road. |
| F4 | 210-261 | EF4 | 168-199 | Devastating: Houses leveled; cars thrown and large missiles generated. |
| F5 | 262-317 | EF5 | 200-234 | Incredible: Automobile-sized missiles fly in excess of 100 meters (109 yards); trees debarked. |

In the United States, most tornado storms travel diagonally from the southwest to the northeast. On the ground, tornadoes usually move in small, **elliptical** (oval-shaped) circles. The path of a tornado, if viewed from an airplane, looks as if someone placed the point of a pencil down on a sheet of paper and made spiral designs across the page. A common tornado will loop forward, turn back, cross its own path, loop forward again, and continue in that manner. This random movement is why a tornado can destroy two houses but leave the one between them untouched.

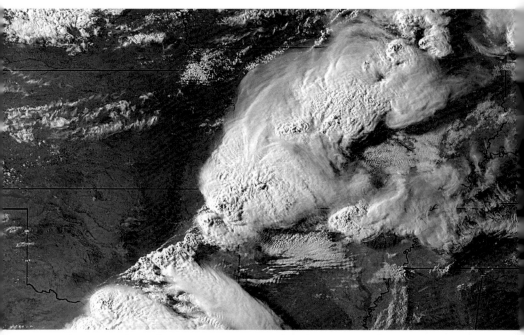

Storm clouds pass over Joplin (center of image) just before the F5 tornado touched down.

Tornadoes occur most often between 3 p.m. and 9 p.m., although they can happen at any time.

Most tornadoes do not stay in one place for very long. They touch down in one area for one or two minutes, and then they spin off to another. Tornadoes also may skip or hop. They have been known to skip over houses and leave them undamaged.

Tornadoes move along the ground at an average speed of 20 to 40 mph (32 to 64 kmh). Some tornadoes can move at speeds of up to 60 mph (96.5 kmh). They can travel along the ground anywhere from a few hundred feet to more than 100 miles (161 km).

In 2007, after studying tornado damage reports, the original Fujita scale was revised to better represent the power of tornadoes and the damage they cause. The Enhanced Fujita scale still rates tornadoes from 0 to 5, but the wind-speed cutoffs are different.

Two women sit among the wreckage in Murphysboro, Illinois, in 1925.

The Weather Channel used fatality statistics and damage reports to rank the ten worst tornadoes in U.S. history.

1. **The Tri-State Tornado (Missouri, Illinois, Indiana); March 18, 1925** Almost seven hundred died in three states.

2. **St. Louis, Missouri; May 27, 1896** More than eight thousand buildings were damaged, 255 died.

3. **Joplin, Missouri; May 22, 2011** This EF5 storm lasted 38 minutes and killed 158.

**4. Tuscaloosa, Alabama; April 27, 2011**
A total of 39 died in the storm's 80-mile (129 km) path.

**5. St. Louis, Missouri; September 29, 1927** In what was dubbed "four terrible minutes," 72 died.

**6. Gainesville, Georgia; April 6, 1936**
Sixty people died in the Cooper Pants factory, the most in one building in U.S. history.

**7. Worcester, Massachusetts; June 9, 1953**
New England's most destructive tornado killed nearly a hundred people.

**8. Hackleburg, Alabama; April 27, 2011**
More than $1 billion in damages and 72 deaths occurred.

**9. Natchez, Mississippi; May 7, 1840**
This F5 tornado killed more than 300, although slave deaths were not recorded.

**10. Waco and Wichita Falls, Texas; May 9-11, 1953, and April 10, 1979**
This tie in Lone Star State disasters killed 159 combined.

Tornado damage in Moore, Oklahoma, topped $2 billion.

This is why tornadoes are now reported as EF5 instead of F5.

Using the Enhanced Fujita scale, scientists have determined that about 70 percent of tornadoes are of EF0 or EF1 intensity. These are called weak tornadoes, lasting anywhere from sixty seconds to just under twenty minutes. Less than 5 percent of tornado deaths are caused by weak tornadoes.

Strong tornadoes (EF2 and EF3) account for 29 percent of all tornadoes. These storms may last from twenty minutes to just under an hour and are responsible for 30 percent of tornado-related deaths.

Only 2 percent of all tornadoes are violent tornadoes (EF4 or EF5). These powerful storms can last for an hour or more. Although violent tornadoes rarely occur, they are responsible for 70 percent of all tornado deaths.

A supercell forms over Booker, Texas, in 2013.

The tornado that struck Moore, Oklahoma, covered a wide area.

# CHAPTER THREE

# PREDICTING TORNADOES

Two years after the devastating Joplin tornado, the city of Moore, Oklahoma, also felt the wrath of a twister. An EF5 tornado ravaged 17 miles (27 km) of the city, killing twenty-four people and causing more than $2 billion in property damage.

With each catastrophic event, such as the ones in Moore and Joplin, as well as the brutal 2011 outbreak in Alabama and other states, people look to meteorologists and other scientists hoping they can better predict such storms and provide warnings of what is to come.

## *Forecasting Tornadoes*

Meteorologists study weather patterns to try to predict when tornadoes may occur. Of the sixteen million thunderstorms that strike Earth every year, fewer than two thousand will result in tornadoes. Tornadoes are hard to predict, but there are methods that meteorologists can use to make their predictions more accurate.

A mobile Doppler radar is used to measure a tornado.

## *Monitoring Tornadic Thunderstorms*

Meteorologists pay attention to the size and shape of developing thunderstorms. Tornadic thunderstorms, the storms strong enough to produce tornadoes, usually have a specific anvil-shape. This means the bottom and the top of the storm are wide and flat, and its middle is thin. If a bubble is sticking out of the flat top of a storm cloud, it means there is a lot of high air pressure and violent wind activity inside the storm. When a storm has this shape and size, a tornado may be forming.

## RAINING FISH

Tornadoes are one type of **whirlwind**. Another is a **waterspout**, which can reach speeds of 200 mph (322 kmh). Waterspouts are more damaging to marine life than people. In 2005, a couple in Folsom, California, reported that it was raining fish, after a waterspout sucked up fish and dropped them onto land.

## Forecasting Tornadoes with Doppler Radar

The most effective tool in forecasting tornadoes is **Doppler radar**. It has been used to detect major storms and tornadoes since

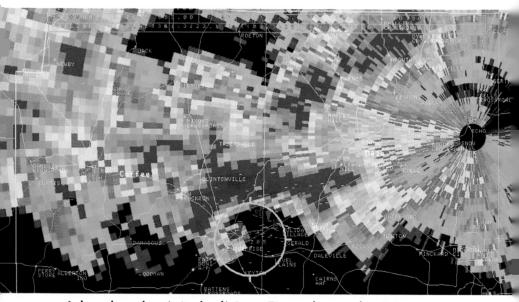

A hook echo (circled) in a Doppler radar image can indicate swirling winds and a tornado.

1971. Doppler radar records the location and strength of storm systems. It tracks wind speed, records shifts in wind activity, and measures rain, snow, and **hail** carried by winds. Shifting winds are thought to be the first sign that a tornado may form.

Doppler radar works by sending out radio waves from an antenna. These waves are reflected back to the antenna by objects in the air, which can include precipitation. Frequency differences, based on whether an object is moving away from or toward the antenna, can be detected. A lower frequency means an object is moving away.

The radar can also detect rotation in the clouds. This means there is a tornado over that area even if it hasn't yet touched ground. If this rotation is detected, the National Weather Service will issue a tornado warning.

## Studying Lightning to Predict Tornadoes

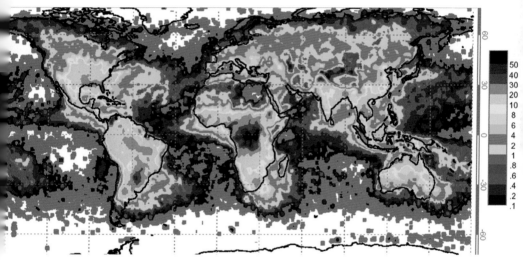

This worldwide map shows lightning flashes annually per square kilometer. Lightning in thunderstorms is used to predict tornadoes.

A more recent advance in predicting tornadoes is the study of lightning. In 1995, the National Aeronautics and Space Administration (NASA) began recording how often lightning occurred in thunderstorms. Lightning was measured by a low-flying satellite called an **Optical Transient Detector (OTD)**. Using the OTD, scientists were able to record the number of lightning flashes in a certain area. Meteorologists now know that tornadoes are formed by the same conditions that produce large amounts of lightning in a storm. They observe the amount of lightning in a storm to help them predict tornadoes.

## Tornado Preparedness

The chance that you will experience a tornado is slim. Even in areas with heavy tornado activity, a tornado isn't likely to strike any one place more than once in every 250 years. Here are a few tips on preparing for a tornado:

- Know your community's warning system.
- Know the difference between a tornado warning and a tornado watch. A tornado watch means that a tornado is possible in your area. A tornado warning is issued when a tornado has actually been spotted and is headed toward the area.
- If you live in an area where tornadoes commonly occur, pack an emergency kit and make a family plan for how you will

Parents should talk to their children about safety plans in case of a tornado.

get to a safe place. Know where the "safe room" is in your house. It should be a storm cellar or an interior room on the lowest floor with no windows.

• If the weather turns, follow the local news or the National Weather Service via television, radio, or the Internet. Make sure there is a radio with plenty of batteries in your emergency kit.

• Move or tie down lawn furniture or anything that can be blown through the air.

A tornado can hit quickly and sometimes without notice. Make sure you are ready to seek shelter as quickly as possible. Visit ready.gov/tornadoes for more information.

Tim Samaras was killed when a tornado overcame his storm chase vehicle.

In the spring of 1994 and 1995, scientists carried out a daring project called VORTEX. Using cars equipped with radar systems, the scientists drove near, in, and around severe thunderstorms. They recorded the temperature, humidity, and wind speed inside the storms. They used the radar to observe the storm's internal shifting winds.

In addition, two planes with radar systems scanned the tops of the storms.

The information gathered was used to create a computer model of a tornado. VORTEX data has helped scientists to better understand the weather conditions present when a tornado forms. This was followed by a second project, VORTEX2 in 2009 and 2010. These studies expanded our knowledge of how tornadoes form and how to better forecast them.

Storm chasers, like those in the VORTEX project, have been romanticized in film and television. The 1996 film *Twister* portrayed the rivalry between two storm-chasing teams. The Discovery Channel aired a reality program called *Storm Chasers* that ran for five seasons.

This work can be dangerous. In June 2013, three veteran storm chasers—Tim Samaras, his son Paul Samaras, and their chase partner Carl Young—were killed in Reno, Oklahoma. A multiple-vortex tornado changed direction and overtook the chasers' vehicle.

# GLOSSARY

**air pressure**  The weight of an air mass in the atmosphere pressing down on any one spot.

**atmosphere**  The thin layer of air surrounding Earth.

**condense**  To change from a gas into a liquid.

**Doppler radar**  Radar that detects and measures precipitation and wind activity.

**elliptical**  Movement that traces the shape of an oval.

**F-Scale**  The scale of measurement that classifies tornadoes according to their wind speeds.

**funnel** Rapidly spinning winds that form the center of a tornado.

**hail** Pellets of frozen rain that fall from clouds.

**humidity** The amount of water vapor in the atmosphere.

**jet stream** A weather pattern of strong winds and low air pressure.

**meteorologist** Scientist who studies weather and climates.

**multi-vortex tornado** A tornado that has two or more small funnels inside a main funnel.

**National Weather Service (NWS)** A U.S. government agency responsible for observing and forecasting weather.

**Optical Transient Detector (OTD)** A low-flying satellite that detects lightning in storms.

**outbreak** A storm that produces several tornadoes in the same area at the same time.

**tornadic thunderstorm** A severe thunderstorm capable of producing a tornado.

**Tornado Alley** An area in the middle of the United States where tornadoes are most common.

**tornado warning** An announcement that a tornado has been seen.

**tornado watch** An announcement that conditions exist for a tornado to form.

**updraft** Strong winds that flow from the ground into the clouds.

**vacuum** An area from which air has been removed, drawing objects into it.

**waterspout** A tornado that happens over a body of water.

**whirlwind** Any storm with strong, swirling winds.

# FURTHER INFORMATION

## Books

Carson, Mary Kay. *Inside Tornadoes*. New York, NY: Sterling Publishing, 2011.

Dougherty, Terri. *The Worst Tornadoes of All Time. Epic Disasters*. Amite, LA: Edge Books, 2012.

Miller, Ron. *Chasing the Storm: Tornadoes, Meteorology, and Weather Watching*. Minneapolis, MN: Twenty First Century Books, 2014.

Sandlin, Lee. *Storm Kings: The Untold History of America's First Tornado Chasers*. New York, NY: Vintage, 2013.

## National Geographic's Tornado Information Page

environment.nationalgeographic.com/
environment/natural-disasters/tornado-
profile

Get safety tips, view videos of tornadoes and profiles of tornado chasers. Check out games and brainteasers to test your knowledge of tornadoes.

## Ready.gov Tornado Preparedness Website

www.ready.gov/tornadoes

This government website helps families understand the risks associated with tornadoes and provides tips on how to deal with outbreaks.

**The Weather Channel's Storm Encyclopedia**
www.weather.com/encyclopedia/tornado/form.html

Learn more about how tornadoes form, how the Fujita scale works, the difference between tornado watches and warnings, and the forecasting of tornadoes.

# INDEX

Page numbers in **boldface** are illustrations.